This book is dedicated to the millions of children around the world who are all different but yet the same.

MY SKIN HAS
SHAPES

BY RAYNA BEST

My skin is very special, it has two different colors. It makes me stand out but they both compliment each other.

Some parts are light and some are not.
I'm okay with that because I love
my skin a lot!

Every night before bed, I look in the mirror and admire my skin! Daddy comes in and says with a grin, "Mya, It's time for me to tuck you in!"

He tucks me in and hugs me with all his might,
turns off the light and says, "Goodnight!"

When I closed my eyes and started to dream,
the lighter parts of my skin turned into star beams!

I lit up with joy as they sparkled & shined. I was
so happy that they were mine!

Moments later, I was covered in circles
from head to toe.

My nightgown had even bigger circles
that had a wonderful glow.

Then all of a sudden triangles appeared!

They looked like upside down ice cream cones
and that made me smile from ear to ear.

I rushed to the mirror to see the
beautiful sight but the shapes
had turned into white kites!

They were diamonds and they fit
me so well. Four sides shining bright
with their own stories to tell.

Those same four sides shifted into squares. They changed different colors without a moment to spare.

I couldn't believe my eyes. It was so rare!

When I woke up the next morning, the dream seemed so real.

I knew in that moment that my skin
is a very big deal.

I may look different from others but there's magic in me.

My skin has shapes and for that,
I am as lucky as can be.

Rayna Best is a wife, mother of three, author and a former educator. During her time working with inner city youth, she discovered her passion for uplifting children within the community. Now, her mission is to empower other children around the world, while spreading awareness about their unique needs and personalities. Her very first book is called, Animated Like Me, which addresses the harsh realities of struggling with inclusion, self acceptance, all while balancing ADHD. She believes that it is her divine gift and purpose to write stories that will evoke change.

Animated Like Me, tells the touching tale of Kamron,
an energetic zebra with ADHD who finds it difficult to
fit in and make friends. Amid this challenging time for him,
he meets Kamille, who also feels like an outcast.
She teaches Kamron the true meaning of friendship,
and together, they show their peers the wonders
of being utterly unique.

CPSIA information can be obtained
at www.ICGtesting.com
Printed in the USA
BVHW022107230421
605722BV00013B/1821